W9-CSB-645

RIGBY

On Our Way to English®

Student Anthology

Rigby®
HOUGHTON MIFFLIN HARCOURT

ISBN 10:   1-418-98536-8
ISBN 13: 978-1-418-98536-3

Printed in China

1 2 3 4 5 6 7 8 0940 15 14 13 12 11 10 09

Contents

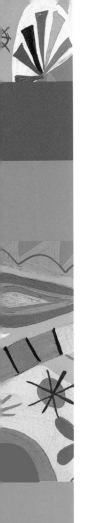

Contents

Faces and Places

THE BIG QUESTION

How are the people and places in our world alike and different?

UNIT 1 Main Selection

Big Book: *Now We Live in the U.S.A.!*

Genre: Personal Narrative

This selection is a **personal narrative**. Personal narratives are stories that people write to tell what happened to them.

Comprehension Strategy: Make Connections

Think about what you are reading and how it connects to what you know and what you have already read. When you **make connections**, you will better understand what you are reading.

Now We Live in the U.S.A. !

Aurora Colón García

New Friends in San Antonio

San Antonio is a city in Texas in the southern part of the United States. A river runs through the heart of the city, and people like to shop and eat on the River Walk there.

Schools in San Antonio have students who come from countries all over the world. My, Guillermo, Wen, and Fernando were born in other countries but now live here in San Antonio, Texas.

Where Were Our Friends Born?

Guillermo

Pacific Ocean

NORTH AMERICA

Atlantic Ocean

MEXICO

N W E S

PERU

SOUTH AMERICA

Fernando

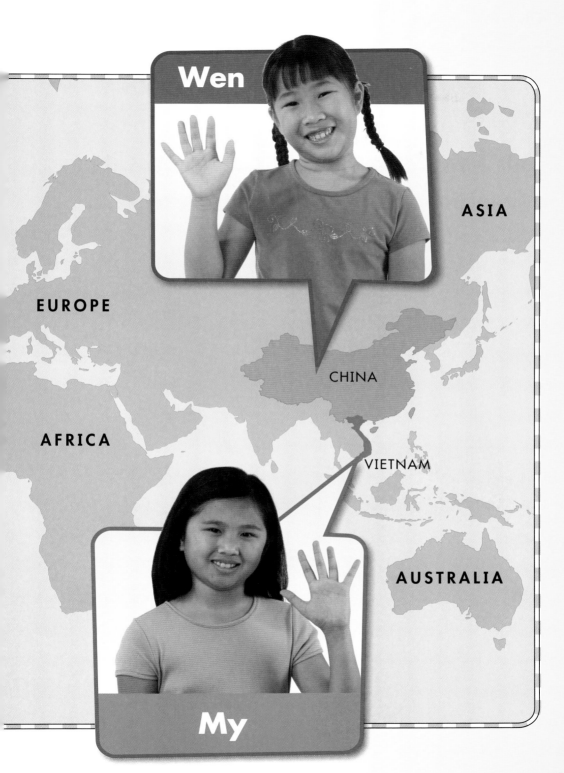

13

Meet My

Hello, my name is My. I speak Vietnamese. I live in the U.S.A. now, but I was born in Ho Chi Minh City, Vietnam.

ASIA

VIETNAM

•Ho Chi Minh City

This is Ho Chi Minh City, Vietnam,
on the continent of Asia.

15

In Vietnam, I used to love going to the market because there was a lot to see. Most people would walk, but others would take pedicabs to the market. There were hundreds of vendors selling everything you can think of. There were chickens, ducks, freshly caught fish, and lots of fresh, delicious tropical fruit.

pedicab

Meet Guillermo

Hello, my name is Guillermo. My nickname is Memo. I speak Spanish. I live in the U.S.A. now, but I was born in Coahuila, Mexico.

This is Coahuila, Mexico, on the continent of North America.

NORTH AMERICA

Coahuila•

Gulf of Mexico

MEXICO

Pacific Ocean

In Mexico, I loved birthday fiestas. Some of my favorite parts were

- breaking the piñatas.
- playing the game *lotería*.
- drinking Mexican hot chocolate.
- eating tamales.

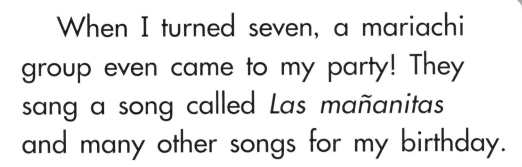

When I turned seven, a mariachi group even came to my party! They sang a song called *Las mañanitas* and many other songs for my birthday.

Meet Wen

Hello, my name is Wen. I speak Mandarin. I live in the U.S.A. now, but I was born in Beijing, China.

你好！我的名字叫王文卿！

This is Beijing, China, on the continent of Asia.

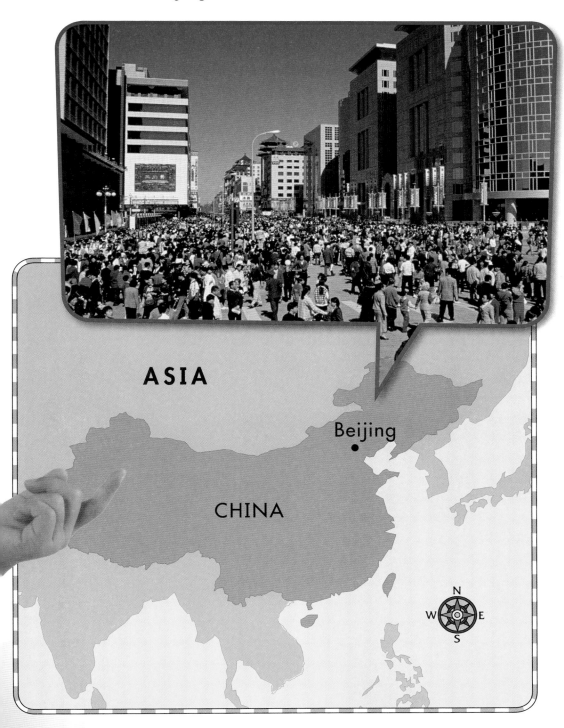

ASIA

Beijing

CHINA

In Beijing, I loved to play Chinese jump rope on the playground. A Chinese jump rope is a loop. It has no ends. Two people stretch it low around their ankles. Then a player jumps in and out of the loop in patterns, sometimes stretching the loop. There are four levels: ankle, knee, waist, and under the shoulder. Speed doesn't matter, but it's fun to jump faster!

ankle

knee

waist

under shoulder

Meet Fernando

Hello, my name is Fernando. I speak Spanish and Quechua, a common Native American language in Peru. I live in the U.S.A. now, but I was born in Lima, Peru.

¡Hola, me llamo Fernando!

sutiymi Fernando

allinllachu

PERU

SOUTH AMERICA

• Lima

This is Lima, Peru, on the continent of South America.

I love to listen to Peruvian music. My father has a Peruvian musical group called Wayanay Inka. The group plays different instruments like quenas, zamponas, and drums. These instruments are made of things like cane, mud, bone, horns, and different metals.

quena

zampoña

What Do We Like Best About the United States?

amusement parks!

field trips to museums!

pizza!

playing basketball!

31

Index

Ho Chi Minh City, Vietnam

My

San Antonio, U.S.A.

Coahuila, Mexico

Guillermo

San Antonio, U.S.A.

Beijing, China

Wen

San Antonio, U.S.A.

Lima, Peru

Fernando

San Antonio, U.S.A.

Crafty Creatures

THE BIG QUESTION

How do animals adapt to the world around them?

Big Book: *The Bird Who Ate Too Much*

Genre: Play

This selection is a **play**. Plays are stories that are written to be acted out for an audience.

Comprehension Strategy: Determine Importance

Think about what you are reading and which parts are important to the story. When you **determine importance**, you identify key details and this helps you better understand the plot.

The Bird Who Ate Too Much

Margarita González-Jensen
Illustrated by Jason Wolff

Act 1

Narrator: A long time ago, a group of birds lived together in a rain forest. It was a wonderful place to live. There was plenty of food to feed them all. One day the birds were sitting in a tree talking about their lunch.

Finch: Those seeds I found were delicious.

Canary: My food was really good, too. And I'm full!

Hummingbird: I ate berries, nuts, and grass seeds. Then I ate more yummy berries for dessert. But I feel like I could eat a horse!

Parakeet trio:
You are hungry, so you say.
But you ate a lot today!

Narrator: Hummingbird was a big, gray bird. He had a beak like the other birds, so he ate everything the other birds ate.

Canary: Hummingbird, how can you still be hungry? I ate less, and I'm so full that I want to nap!

Hummingbird: I could nap or have a light snack first.

Finch: You're the hungriest bird I've ever seen!

Narrator: The next day the birds got together again after lunch—all except for Hummingbird.

Canary: What a terrible day! Most of my favorite food was gone.

Finch: Mine, too. I couldn't find my delicious seeds today. Hummingbird isn't back yet. Maybe he found some good food to eat.

Parakeet trio:
Something bad is going on.
All our favorite food is gone!

Narrator: The birds flew off to find Hummingbird because they suspected that he might know where the food was. Soon they returned one by one.

Finch: I didn't find Hummingbird, but I discovered something strange.

Canary: What did you discover?

Finch: Not only is our food gone, but so are the flowers. Someone's even eaten the petals, buds, and pollen!

Narrator: As the birds ruffled their feathers and squawked, no one noticed Hummingbird returning to his nest. His beak and belly were stained and covered with pollen. He quickly fell asleep.

Parakeet trio:

All the food is gone. It's true.
Even all the flowers, too!

Act II

Narrator: As the hungry birds discussed what to do, Butterfly flew to Queen Quetzal.

Butterfly: Dear Queen, someone is destroying our food and flowers! I saw it all.

Queen Quetzal: What do you know, Butterfly?

Butterfly: A bird in our valley ate all the berries and seeds and then all the flowers, too!

Parakeet Trio:
*Butterfly will help us find out
Who's been sneaking about.*

Narrator: At that moment, the others went to Queen Quetzal.

Finch: Dear Queen, our food is disappearing, and we're hungry.

Queen Quetzal: Yes, I have been told about a bird that is causing the problem.

Finch: Please tell us who he is.

Queen Quetzal: Butterfly, who is this bird?

Butterfly: I don't know him, but his gray feathers are stained with the color of flowers.

Narrator: Suddenly Hummingbird flew nearby. His feathers were covered with pollen and spotted with color.

Butterfly: Stop that bird! He's the one who's eating everything.

Hummingbird: But it's all so delicious.

Queen Quetzal: Hummingbird, since you don't leave food for others, there's only one thing I can do.

Parakeet Trio:
What the Queen will say and do
Will keep our food away from you.

Queen Quetzal:
I will turn you into a tiny bird with a long and narrow beak! You will only be able to drink the flowers' nectar.

Narrator: In the blink of an eye, Hummingbird changed.

Parakeet Trio:
*Now you can't steal
Everyone's meal!*

Narrator: Hummingbird looked at the other birds as his tiny eyes filled with tears. When they saw his sorrow, they showered him with flower petals.

Finch and Canary: May these beautiful colors ease your sorrow!

Narrator: As the petals fell on Hummingbird, his feathers became the brilliant colors of blue, red, yellow, and green flowers in bloom.

Parakeet Trio:
For your greed,
You had to pay.
Now hunger will make
You eat all day.
But don't be sad.
Your feathers are bright,
And you're the most beautiful
Bird in sight!

Problem

Event

Solution

Then and NOW

THE BIG QUESTION

How have new ways of travel changed our lives?

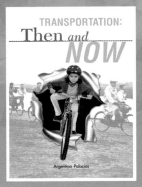

Big Book: *Transportation: Then and Now*

Genre: Expository Text

This selection is expository text. **Expository texts** are stories that people write about what happened to them.

Comprehension Strategy: Monitor Understanding

As you are reading, it helps to check, or monitor, understanding of what you are reading. Stop along the way to figure out whether you understand the text. If understanding breaks down, then reread text you don't understand or ask yourself questions. When you **monitor understanding**, you will be a better reader.

TRANSPORTATION:
Then and
NOW

Argentina Palacios

Introduction

Look in the streets, by the shore, and in the sky. What do you see? You probably see many ways that people move around: bicycles, trains, ships, cars, and planes. People used to walk everywhere, but then they thought of a few new ways to move around.

Bicycles

Can you imagine riding a bicycle without pedals? Long ago there was a wooden bicycle that the rider moved by pushing his feet on the ground.

1817 The hobby horse was invented.

1800

1850

Another bicycle of long ago had a metal frame, wooden wheels, and a front wheel that was taller than you! This bicycle was called the bone shaker. It was very uncomfortable!

1870 The high-wheeler was invented.

1900

Today's bicycles are not as heavy, clumsy, and uncomfortable as the old ones. There are bicycles for racing, for mountain biking, or for just having fun.

1984 Bicyclists prepared for the Summer Olympic Games.

1950

Each type of bike may look different, but they all have the same basic parts that were developed more than 100 years ago: a seat, handlebars, pedals, and brakes.

2001 World Mountain Bike Championships junior downhill races took place.

brakes
handlebars

2000

pedals

Trains

Did you know trains once ran on wooden tracks and were pulled by animals or even people?

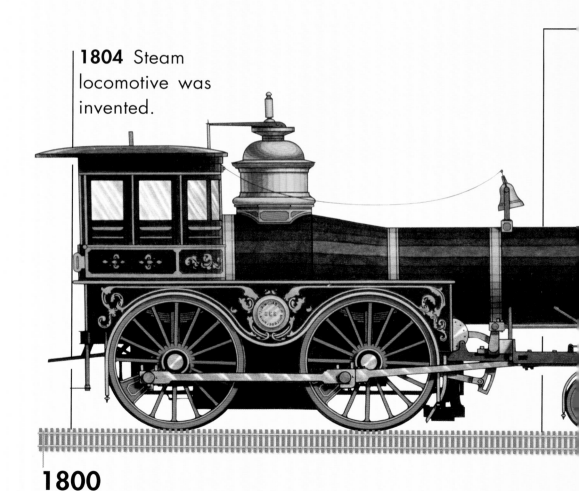

1804 Steam locomotive was invented.

1800

In the 1800s, steam-powered locomotives pulled the first trains. The steam train moved so fast that some people were afraid of them. At that time, a train could go about 20 miles per hour.

1830 A famous race was held between a horse and a steam locomotive.

1869 First transcontinental railroad was completed.

1850

Over time trains became faster and more comfortable. Some cities even built underground train systems called subways.

1897 Boston became the first U.S. city to have a subway.

1900

Improvements are still being made. Maglev trains move as they actually float above a magnetic track. These trains can zoom along at speeds up to 300 miles per hour.

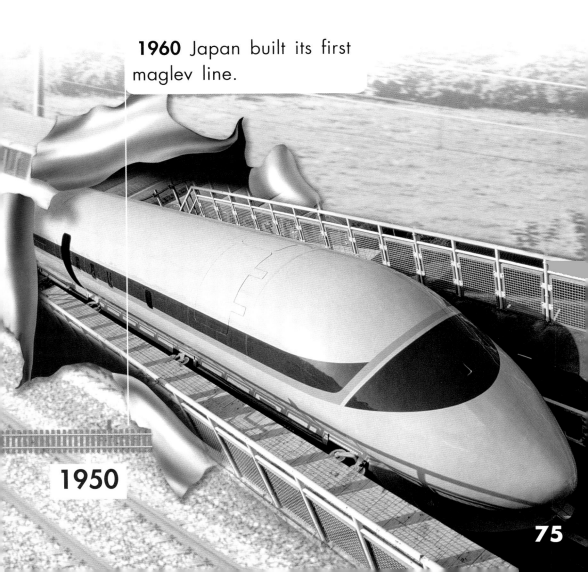

1960 Japan built its first maglev line.

1950

Ships

Have you ever wondered how people traveled by water long ago? Originally people traveled in simple canoes.

300 The Maya lived in Tulum, where they used canoes to transport goods.

793 The first recorded Viking raids occurred in Britain.

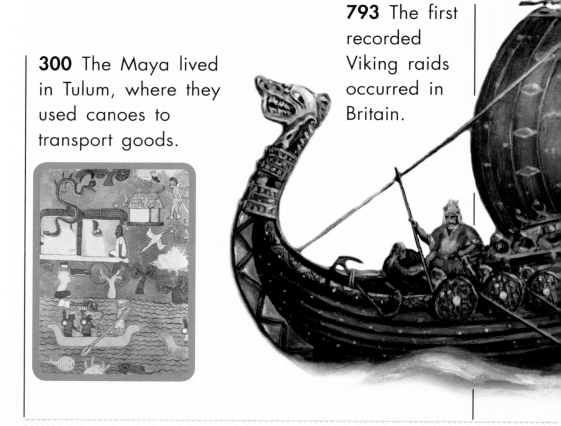

500

Then large boats were built that required many men to row. Ships that needed sails came later. Now when we look at the ships of long ago, we wonder how they ever sailed.

1450 Full-rigged sailing ship was developed.

1000

Water travel really changed when people began using steam-powered ships to take long trips.

1912 The steam-powered Titanic struck an iceberg and sank in the North Atlantic Ocean.

1500

Today's ships are very advanced. Diesel and gas engines power more modern ships, and many use a special kind of energy called nuclear power.

2000 Many U.S. combat warships are nuclear powered.

2000

Cars

Can you imagine riding in a car with only three wheels? At the end of the 19th century, the first automobile looked quite different. It didn't have a roof or windshield, and it only had three wheels.

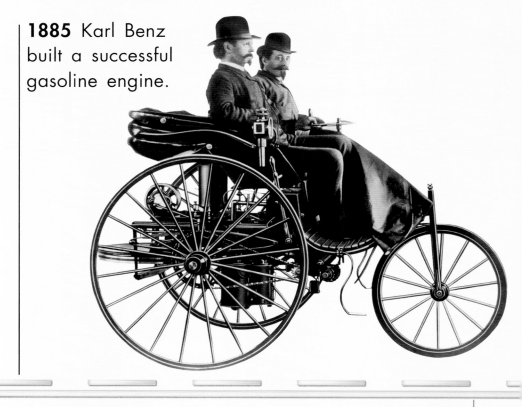

1885 Karl Benz built a successful gasoline engine.

1880

1900

Early cars were very expensive because they were made by hand. Then someone had the idea to use an assembly line to put cars together, and they became much more affordable.

1908
Henry Ford introduced the Model T automobile.

1914 Henry Ford established the first moving assembly line.

1920

Many new vehicles have resulted from the invention of the car. Specialized vehicles now serve different purposes:

1950s Red double-decker buses were popular in London.

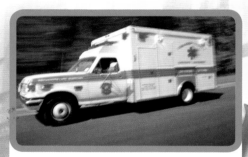

1997 An ambulance helped to save Detroit Lions' football player Reggie Brown.

1940

1960

- Buses for public transportation
- Ambulances for taking people to the hospital
- Fire trucks for fighting fires

2001 Over 100 fire trucks came to the rescue at the World Trade Center on September 11, 2001.

1980

2000

Airplanes

Have you ever wanted to fly? Some people have always had the desire to soar above the clouds. The first flights were in hot-air balloons and gliders. It is believed people in ancient times tried to build kites strong enough to lift a person.

1783 First hot-air balloon flight.

1800

1850

Eventually in 1903 two brothers made an airplane that stayed in the air for 12 seconds. That airplane didn't look like the planes we have today, but it made us believe that flying was possible.

1891 First glider flight.

1903 Wright brothers built the Flyer.

Wilbur and Orville Wright

1900

Flying is the fastest way to travel these days. In fact, some airplanes can fly faster than the speed of sound!

1969 The Concorde made its first test flight.

1937 Amelia Earhart attempted to fly around the world.

1950

Whether you choose to travel by plane, train, ship, or bicycle, one thing is for sure—there are plenty of different ways to get around!

1981 The first space shuttle blasted off.

2000

Glossary

assembly line – a row of machines and people working together to make a product

diesel engine – an engine that uses diesel fuel to make it go

glider – an aircraft without an engine

locomotive – the train engine that pushes or pulls a train

Index

Then		Now

Then   **Now**

 bicycles

 trains

 ships

 cars

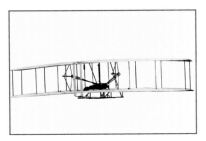 airplanes

Making Life Easier

THE BIG QUESTION

How has technology changed our world?

UNIT 4 Main Selection

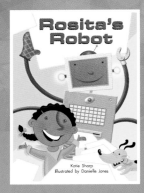

Big Book: *Rosita's Robot*

Genre: Science Fiction

This selection is **science fiction**. Science fiction is a form of fantasy that is set in a future world. In science fiction stories, events can be explained by science, and people usually use science to solve problems.

Comprehension Strategy: Create Sensory and Emotional Images

As you are reading, it helps to create pictures in your mind that relate to your senses and feelings. That is, ask yourself how the text shows us—rather than tells us—something. When you **create sensory and emotional images**, you will get the most out of your reading.

Rosita's Robot

Katie Sharp
Illustrated by Danielle Jones

Rosita's mother gave her chores to do around the house. But whenever her mother handed her a list, Rosita would find something else to keep her busy. Rosita just wanted to have fun.

Rosita's Chores

☐ Do Homework
☐ Feed Sparky
☐ Clean Room

Grocery List
Milk
Bread
Apples

Each day Rosita's friends would come to the door and ask her to play outside.

Rosita had not done her work, but she still asked, "Mom, can I go and play?"

Rosita's Chores
☐ Do Homework
☐ Feed Sparky
☐ Clean Room

Before Rosita could walk out
through the door, her mother told her,
*"You should get your work done,
And THEN you can have
some fun."*

Rosita thought about how she could get her work done faster. She had an idea. A robot could help her! She gathered old computers, a telescope, and other gadgets.

Rosita's mother called out to her,
*"You should get your work done,
And THEN you can have
some fun."*

At last Rosita built her robot, and it looked like this:

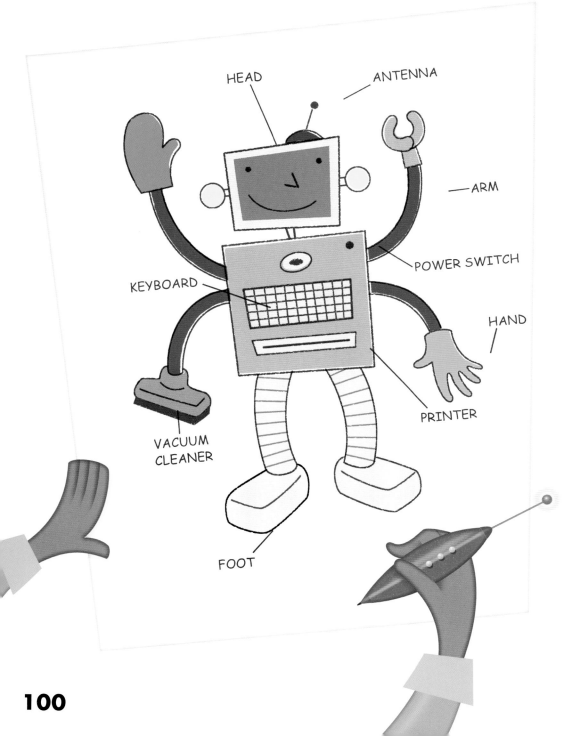

To make her robot work, Rosita gave it a command.

"Let's play a game," she said.

Much to her surprise, the robot told her,

"You should get your work done,
And THEN you can have
some fun."

"OK, robot," Rosita said, "I have to hit the books now. Let's do my moon report."

Rosita was able to look through the robot's telescope and see the big, round moon.

"I can see the man in the moon!" Rosita exclaimed.

"Light and shadows on mountains, valleys, rocks, and craters make the face you see," the robot told her.

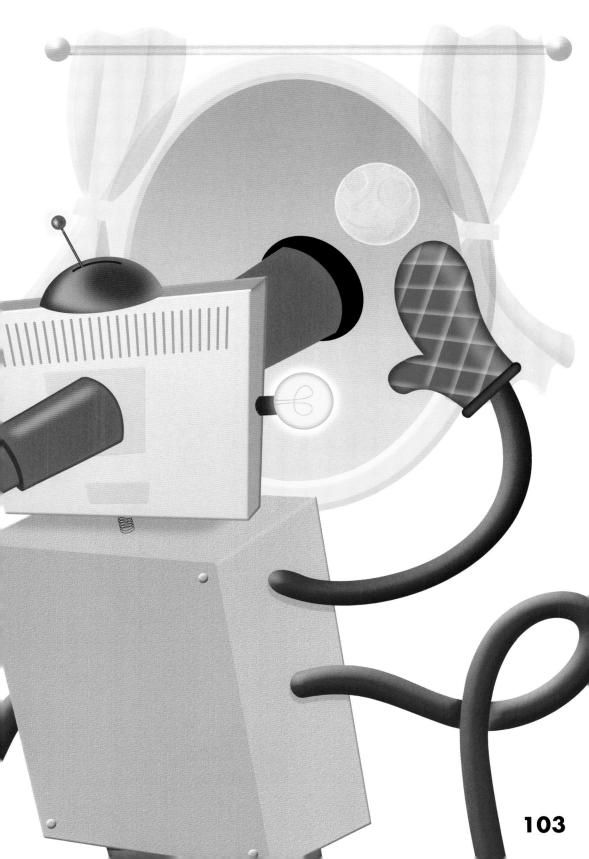

As Rosita learned more about the moon, she told her robot what to write. Soon pages and pages of her report were printing out of the robot's body.

With her report finished, Rosita wanted to take a trip. "Robot, let's go to the moon," she said.

The robot told her,

"You should get your work done,
And THEN you can have
some fun."

Rosita's Chores
☑ Do Homework
☐ Feed Sparky
☐ Clean Room

The Moon

Suddenly Rosita heard her dog
barking, and saw him running to her.
"It must be time to feed Sparky,"
she said.

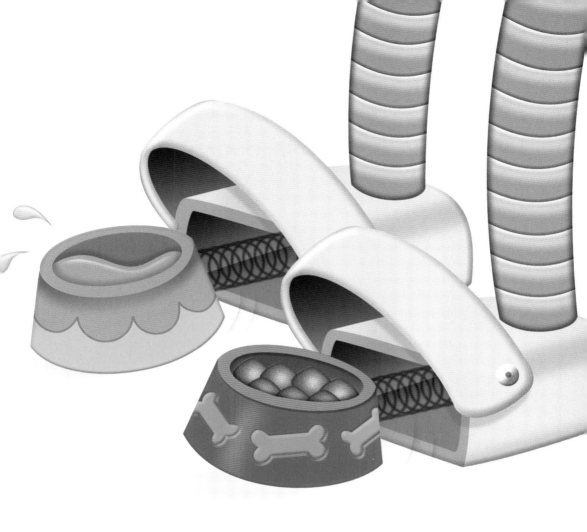

"Robot, give Sparky his water and food," Rosita commanded.

At once, two dog bowls slid out of the robot's feet. One bowl was filled with water. The other had food.

Sparky quickly ate his food and finished his water. Then he took a red ball in his mouth and brought it to Rosita.

"Robot, let's play with Sparky,"
Rosita said.
The robot just shook its head,
"You should get your work done,
And THEN you can have
some fun."

Rosita's Chores
☑ Do Homework
☑ Feed Sparky
☐ Clean Room

Rosita looked at her list and said, "I have just one more thing to do."

She led her robot to her room and they looked around.

"My room is a mess," Rosita said. "Robot, clean my room!"

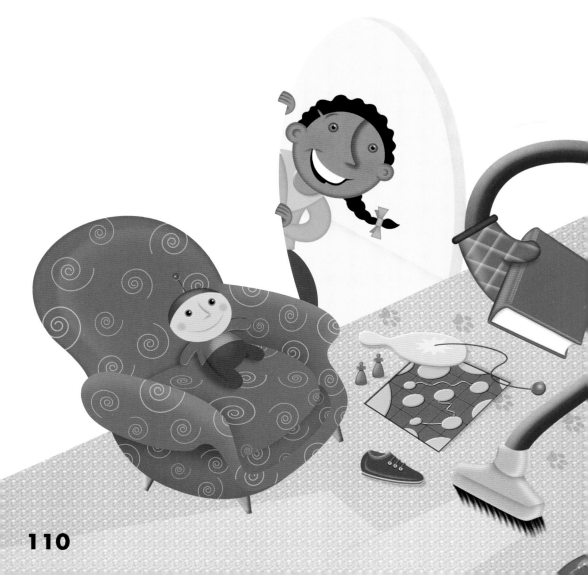

Within seconds, the robot was at work. All at once, it made Rosita's bed, put away the toys and books, and neatly folded all her clothes.

Then the robot vacuumed the rug and curtains. With another arm, it washed the windows. And with yet two other arms, it carefully cleaned the hamster's cage.

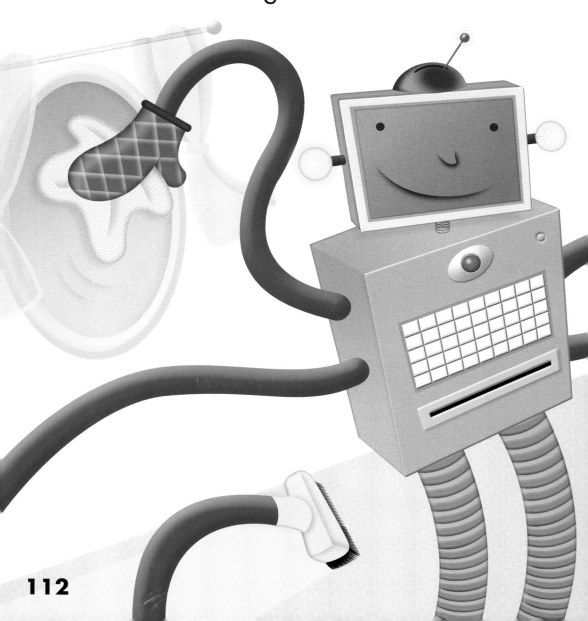

Rosita, dizzy from watching her
robot work, smiled and said,
"Now that my work is done,
I can go and have some fun!"

Rosita turned off her robot and ran to the door. She was finally going to have some fun! She grabbed her scooter and helmet.

"Bye, Mom," she called. "I'm going outside to play."

Rosita started to ride her scooter
when suddenly she stopped and said,
"Now that my work is done,
I don't feel like going out for fun."

Rosita ran back, turned the robot
on again, and whispered,
  "I don't want my work to be done,
  Because spending time with you is
    so much fun!"

work to do

robot

do homework

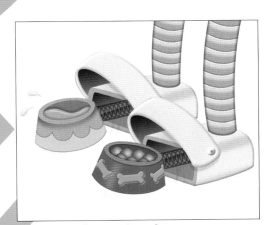

feed dog

clean room

fun working
with robot

Shoot
for the
Stars

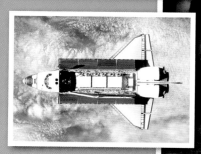

Why is it important to learn about the universe? How do we explore it?

Big Book: *Future Space Explorers: The Ultimate Camp Adventure*

Genre: Expository Text

This selection is **expository text**. Expository texts provide information about a topic. In an expository text, the information is organized in a clear way.

Comprehension Strategy: Infer

As you are reading, it helps to think about any background information you already know about the topic. This helps you fill in the gaps in a text. When you **infer**, you use what you know to better understand what you read.

Future Space Explorers:

The Ultimate Camp Adventure

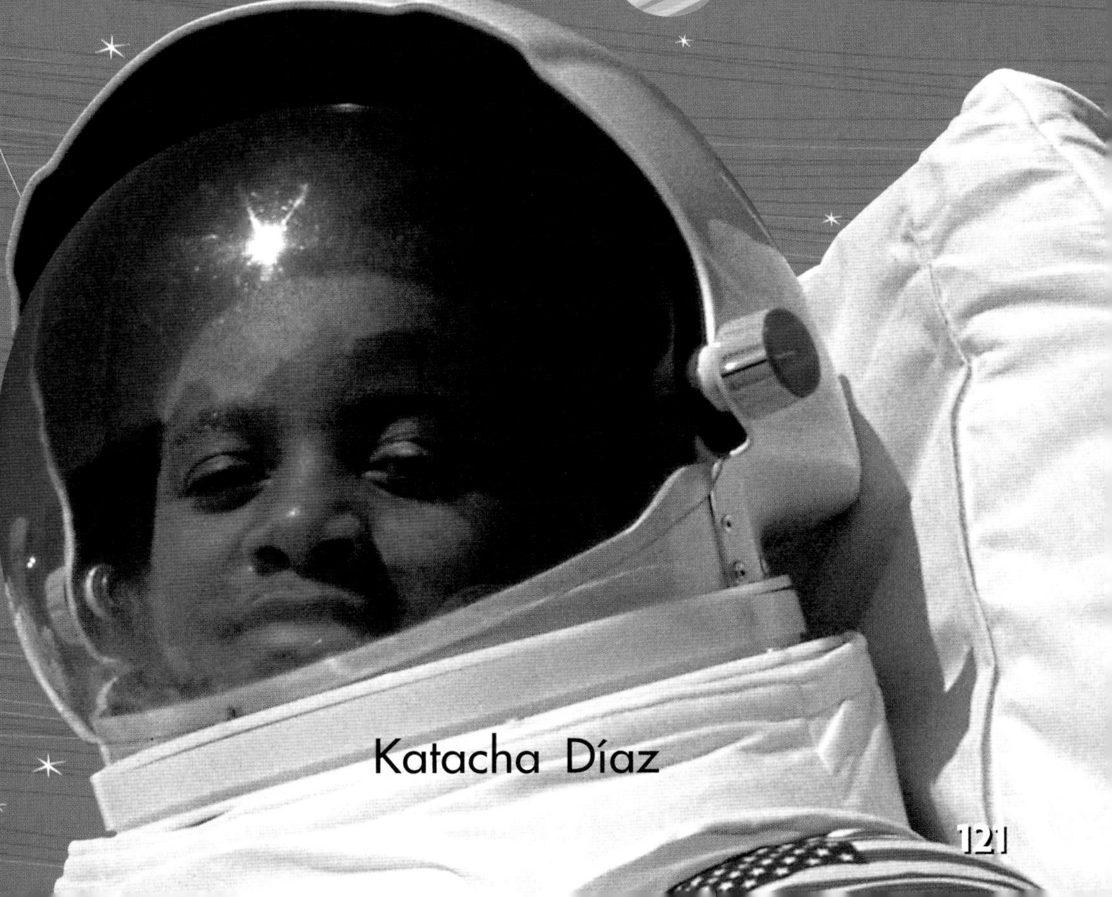

Katacha Díaz

ASTRONAUT TRAINING

Welcome to the NASA Johnson Space Center in Houston, Texas. This is where future astronauts come to take special classes and learn about space.

NASA stands for National Aeronautics and Space Administration

Thousands of men and women apply for the job, but NASA only chooses a few to train. Astronaut trainees learn what it's like to travel, live, work, and float in space.

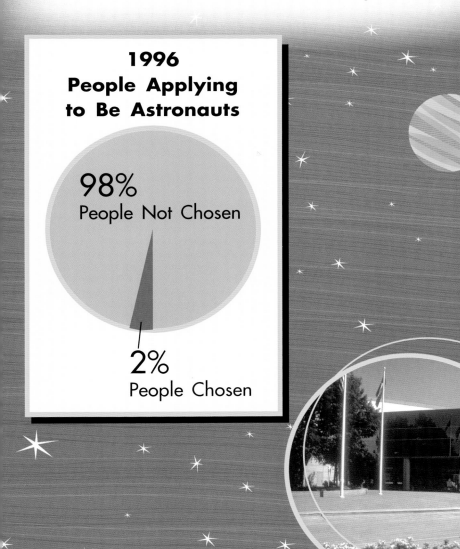

1996
People Applying
to Be Astronauts

98%
People Not Chosen

2%
People Chosen

Did you ever think about becoming an astronaut? Then the U.S. Space Camp in Huntsville, Alabama, is just the place for you!

Thousands of kids visit every year and spend one week training in the world-famous Space Camp. Every boy and girl who attends wants to learn what it takes to be a NASA astronaut.

FLOATING IN SPACE

When up in space, astronauts. experience something unusual—they float. That's because there is almost no gravity in space. This is called zero gravity.

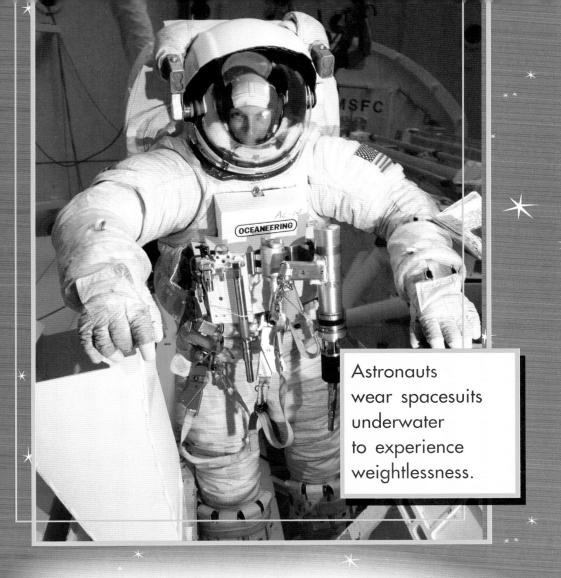

Astronauts wear spacesuits underwater to experience weightlessness.

There is no up or down in space. So men and women astronauts must train to work in weightless conditions. Special water tanks allow them to experience what weightlessness feels like.

Since children want to know how it feels for real astronauts to work while floating, junior astronauts in Huntsville practice being weightless, too.

Experiencing a lack of gravity in the buoyancy tank at Space Camp

Junior astronauts take turns trying out the moon gravity chair. Like the NASA astronauts, these future space explorers experience what it would be like if they were one-sixth of their actual weight.

Feeling weightless in the moon gravity chair at Space Camp

GLIDING IN
THE AIR

Astronauts also train on the equipment that they will be using in space. The Manned Maneuvering Unit, or MMU, allows astronauts to fly free in space without being attached to the shuttle.

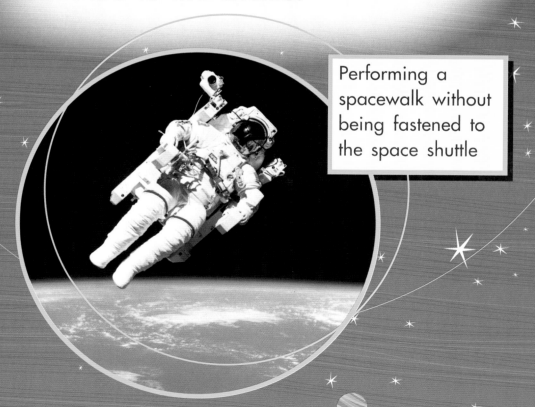

Performing a spacewalk without being fastened to the space shuttle

On Earth astronauts train with the MMU under water so that they have an idea how it will feel to work with the unit in space.

In water and in space, they feel like they're floating weightless.

Using the MMU in underwater training

Junior astronauts try out the MMU. This equipment gives children an opportunity to move in any direction or even go around in a complete circle by moving switches.

Later they will also train under water in a large pool. They'll swim through hoops and experience what it's like to enter the spacecraft and practice using emergency exits.

Using the MMU at Huntsville Space Camp

LIVING IN SPACE

The crew quarters are like a nice, cozy cabin on Earth. They have storage space, stereo headsets, TVs, VCRs, a bathroom, and sleeping bags.

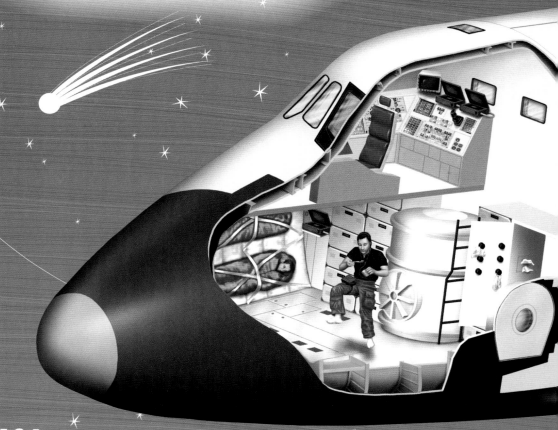

When it's time to sleep, astronauts climb into sleeping bags fastened to the wall. There are even straps to hold them in place. If there weren't, the astronauts would float away while they were sleeping.

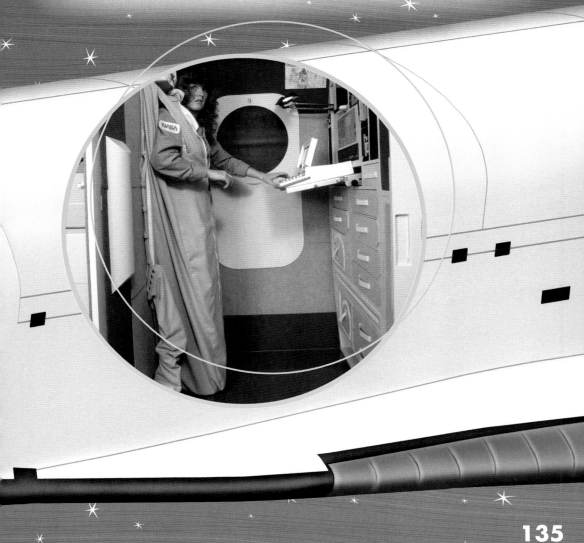

Junior astronauts explore pretend living quarters at Space Camp. The kids get a chance to see what it's like to live in a small and compact place, just like the NASA astronauts do when they're in space.

Junior astronauts visit the kitchen area, exercise area, and bathroom, and also take turns climbing into the sleeping bags.

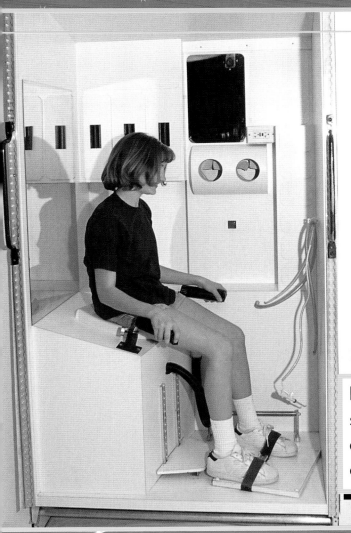

Exploring the shower, bathroom, and sleeping bags at Space Camp

CLOTHES AND UNIFORMS

NASA uniforms and clothing are designed so that astronauts can do their work comfortably. Astronauts working inside the spacecraft wear pants and knit shirts or flight suits.

Astronauts who work outside the spacecraft wear space suits and helmets. They get extra training, too. These astronauts practice how to do their work wearing bulky space suits.

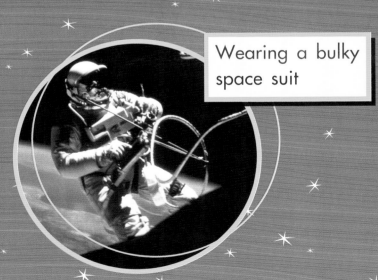

Wearing a bulky space suit

Junior astronauts wear comfortable clothes, too. They wear official Space Camp T-shirts and visors. They even learn about astronauts' space suits.

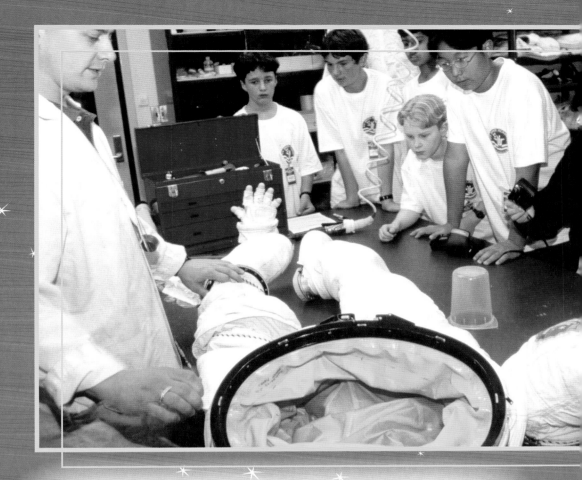

On Mission Day, some kids actually have a chance to try on NASA-style flight suits while others suit up in bulky space suits and helmets. It all depends on the job they're doing that day. One thing is for sure—they all are decked out like real NASA astronauts!

FUTURE SPACE EXPLORERS

The men and women trainees at the NASA Johnson Space Center dream of one day becoming astronauts, just like some of the kids at Space Camp. The astronauts study math and science. Those who really want to fulfill their goals won't let a little hard work spoil their dreams!

Who knows? Maybe some of you will be future space explorers, too!

INDEX

becoming an astronaut

zero
gravity

weightlessness

equipment
training

crew living
quarters

Our Valuable EARTH

What does it mean to "save the planet"?

Big Book: *Diego Saves the Planet!*

Genre: Realistic Fiction

This selection is **realistic fiction.** Realistic fiction texts are stories in which characters act in realistic ways to solve problems. The settings, or location and time, of realistic fiction stories are usually easily recognizable.

Comprehension Strategy: Ask Questions

As you are reading, it helps to keep track of what you wonder about the text. This keeps you focused on the text. **Asking questions** about what you read makes you a better reader.

Diego Saves
the
Planet!

Angela Shelf Medearis
Illustrated by Josée Masse

Every summer Diego visits his *Tía* Mari. He loves to play in the park near her house.

151

But the park looked different
this summer. Newspapers, bottles,
and cans covered the ground.

There were few fish in the creek, and oil was floating on top of the water. There were wilted brown plants where green plants used to sprout.

Diego wondered how the park and creek got so dirty. He saw water flowing from a drainpipe into the creek. Diego followed the drainpipe down the street.

Mr. Ching was fixing his car. The oil from his car was running into the drain.

"So that's where some of the oil is coming from," Diego said.

He told Mr. Ching about the park and the oil in the creek.

"I'm sorry, Diego," said Mr. Ching. "What should we do?"

"Let's put a pan underneath your car to catch the oil," said Diego. "Cleaning up the oil will help save the planet."

"Great idea!" Mr. Ching said.

We each use about 35,000 gallons of water every year.

A bathtub holds 25–30 gallons of water.

Flushing a toilet uses 3–7 gallons of water.

Diego saw Mrs. Peters. She was carrying her recycling bin. A few of her newspapers blew down the street. Diego picked them up.

"So that's how some of the newspapers got into the park," Diego said.

Diego told Mrs. Peters about the garbage in the park. "Let's put this rock on top of the newspapers in your recycling bin," Diego said. "Then they won't blow into the park. Recycling helps to save the planet."

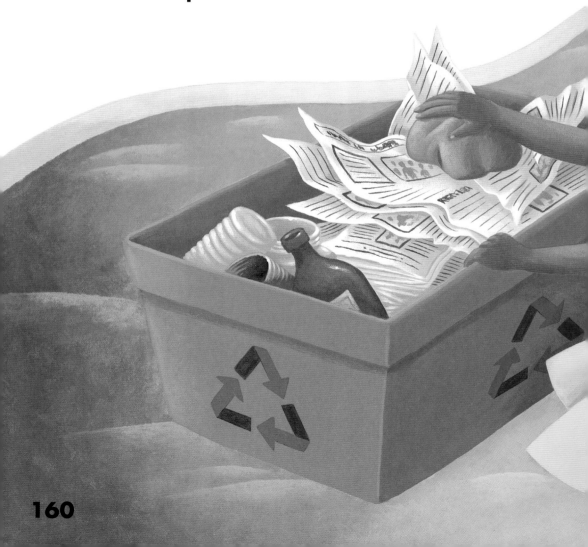

It takes 90% less energy to recycle aluminum cans than to make new ones.

We each produce about 4.6 pounds of garbage every day. Some of it can be recycled.

"Did you have fun at the park?" *Tía* Mari asked Diego.

"No," Diego said. "The creek isn't clean anymore."

"I'm sorry, Diego," *Tía* Mari said. "What can I do to help?"

"Could you put ladybugs on your roses?" Diego asked.

"Ladybugs!" *Tía* Mari said. "How will ladybugs help clean the creek?"

"The chemicals you're using flow into the drain. Then they go into the creek," Diego said. "Ladybugs will eat some of the bugs on your roses. Using ladybugs will help save the planet!"

Aphids are some of the insects that eat plants.

Ladybugs eat aphids, but most ladybugs don't harm plants.

We can use ladybugs instead of chemicals to control insects.

"Tomorrow I'm going to clean up the park," Diego said. "I'll make signs telling everyone how they can keep the park clean."

Diego worked carefully on his signs. He wrote down what Mr. Ching, Mrs. Peters, and *Tía* Mari did to help keep the park clean.

The next day, Diego took his signs to the park. He put them up on the bulletin boards. Then he started to pick up the garbage.

Later everyone in the neighborhood pitched in.

"Now the park and the creek are clean!" Diego said.

"What should we name the park?" Mr. Ching asked.

"How about Planet Park?" Diego said.

"Planet Park is a great name!" said Mr. Ching. "Let's make a sign for our park."

"We should make a sign for the creek, too," Mrs. Peters said.

"Let's call it Diego's Creek!" *Tía* Mari said.

Tía Mari got her camera ready to take a photo of Diego standing next to the new sign at the creek.

"So, Diego, how does it feel to save the planet?" *Tía* Mari asked.

"It feels great!" Diego said.

Problem

Solution

We the People

THE BIG QUESTION

How can we be good citizens?

Big Book: *Making a Difference*

Genre: Story with Procedural Text

Procedural text is a set of directions for making or doing something. This selection is about how a boy and his friends solve a problem. At the end of the story, there are directions for solving problems.

Comprehension Strategy: Use Fix-Up Strategies

When you get stuck on a word or a sentence, use strategies to help you. Use phonics and word study skills, break a word into parts, use picture clues, or read.

Making a
Difference

Patricia Almada
Illustrated by Mike Reed

177

Henry loved the cool breeze rushing past him as he skated. His shiny new wheels were the quickest wheels around. Henry flew through town. His skates were the wings on his feet.

It was a beautiful day and Henry couldn't wait to meet his friends at the park.

Henry arrived at the library and joined his friends Alex, Alicia, and Mark. Before they started to skate, the librarian came out and said, "Not here! You know the rules!"

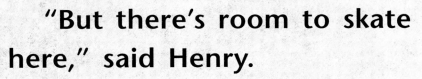

"But there's room to skate
here," said Henry.

"Rules are rules, even if there's
space," the librarian responded.
The kids chanted,
"Not here, not there,
We can't skate anywhere!"
And they skated away.

Soon they were at the park.
They started to skate down a
small path when the park keeper
shouted, "No skating here!"

"But it's early, and no one is here," Henry moaned.

"Rules are rules, even if no one is here," said the park keeper.

The kids chanted,

"*Not here, not there,*

We can't skate anywhere!"

Henry, Alicia, and Alex took
a seat at a nearby bench and
wondered what they could do.
When they noticed Mark drawing
a picture in the sand, they went
over to take a look.

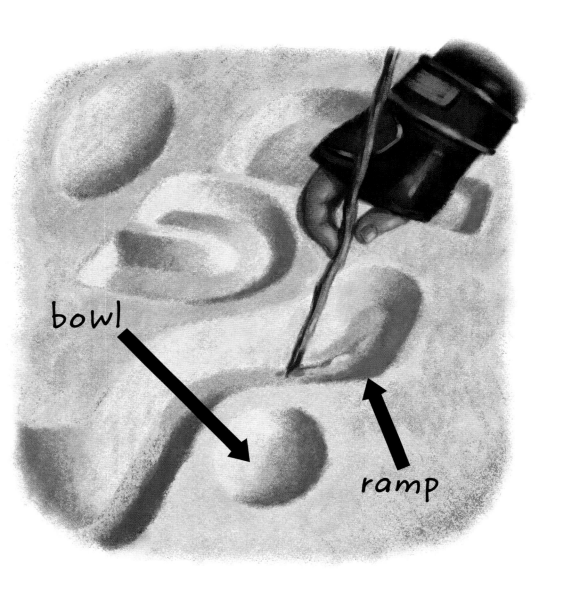

bowl

ramp

"The skate park where I used to live looked like this," Mark said.

"Wow, that looks amazing. I wish we had a skate park here!" said Alicia.

That evening Henry told his parents, "We need a skate park." He showed them his list of the problems the children were having and ideas he had for a solution.

Problem	Solution
• no place to skate	• find a safe place to skate
• we could get hurt	• ask for help
• we are bothering people	

"You can ask the city to build a skate park. Write a speech and present it to the city council," said Mom.

"Don't forget to include good reasons for your ideas," said Dad.

A week later, Henry, his parents, and friends went to the city council meeting.

When his name was called, Henry felt uncertain about whether he had the courage to share his idea. He walked slowly to the podium and read his speech.

Ms. Polynisse   Mr. Ellis   Ms. Sanchez   Mr. Hooper   Ms. Koo

City Council Members:
     I am Henry Parsico. I can't find a place to skate in our city. My friends and I don't want to bother neighbors or break any rules. Please help us by building a skate park so we can skate safely.

Thank you!

"Thank you, Henry. We like to hear from kids because they are important citizens," said the mayor.

"The city council will discuss it and see if we can help. You'll have to be patient. These things take time."

Everyone clapped as Henry walked out. A reporter took his picture and promised to write a story about him. Henry felt wonderful!

"I'm proud of you," said Mom, "You were brave and responsible."

Henry's friends chanted,
"In our city, in our town,
We'll have the best skate
park around!"

You Can Make a Difference!

If you want to change something in your community, you will need to be prepared, be ready to listen, and have patience.

Step 1:

Talk to your friends and brainstorm possible solutions. You will also need the help of responsible adults, so discuss it with your parents or teachers.

Step 2:

Next talk to someone at City Hall. Look for the right person in your city's list of commissions, or ask for a city council member. They will be happy to listen and give you advice.

GOVERNMENT OFFICES

Billing Information	555-0412
City Hall	555-1000
Emergency Services and Disaster	555-1234
Public Works	555-5100
Parks and Recreation Department—	
Recreation Office	555-1586
Building and Zoning	555-7150
City Clerk	555-0812
City Administrator	555-3122
Fire Department	
Emergency	911
Non-Emergency	555-6803

You may be asked to present your idea to a commission or city council. It may take time and compromise, but if your idea is good, the council might do it.

It's kids like you who make a difference in their communities. You can be a hero, too. You can make a difference!

Problem

Think of solutions

Problem	Solution
• no place to skate	• find a safe place to skate
• we could get hurt	• ask for help
• we are bothering people	

Talk with adults

Present your ideas

IN THE MONEY

How do we earn and
spend money?

Big Book: *The Moneybag: a Tale from Korea*

Genre: Folktale

This selection is a folktale—a story that teaches us something. Often characters in **folktales** stand for good and evil. Many different cultures have folktales.

Comprehension Strategy: Synthesize

When you read, you discover different pieces of information, like puzzle pieces. When you put together some of these pieces, you can find a pattern or a bigger picture. This process is called *synthesizing*. When you **synthesize** text, you better understand what you read.

The Moneybag:

A TALE FROM KOREA

Retold by Brenda Parkes
Illustrated by Daniel Powers

Long ago a couple lived in a small hut. Each day they took their axes to the mountain to cut two bundles of firewood.

They left one bundle of firewood in the courtyard to be sold. The other bundle was taken into the kitchen for their own use.

But one morning they woke to find the firewood in the courtyard had disappeared. This went on for three more mornings.

The husband thought that
something fishy was happening.
So the next night he hid inside
the bundle of wood in the
courtyard and waited.

Just before dawn, four tiny
men came and carried the bundle
up the mountain and into a cave.
There a kind-looking old man
untied the bundle to reveal the
woodcutter.

"Tell me, woodcutter," said the old man. "Why is it that everyone else only cuts one bundle of firewood each day, but you and your wife cut two?"

The woodcutter replied, "We are poor, so we cut one bundle to sell and use the other one ourselves."

The old man said, "Because you are hard-working people, I'm going to give you this." He smiled, handing the woodcutter a moneybag.

"You can ask the moneybag for only one silver piece each day. Do this, and your treasure will last all your life."

Suddenly the woodcutter was back in his hut with the moneybag. He told his wife the whole story. She could hardly believe their good fortune.

Every day they still cut two bundles of firewood. Every night they opened the bag and said,

"*Moneybag, Moneybag,*
Give us one silver piece."

And each time, one silver piece would roll out.

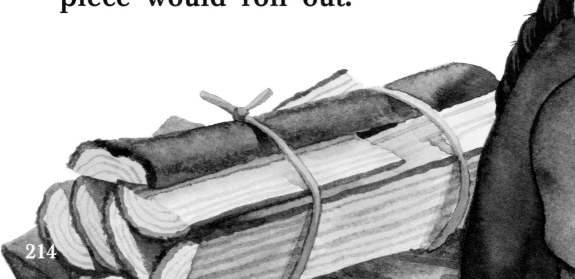

The pile of silver grew high.

"Let's buy an ox to carry the firewood," suggested the husband.

"We should save money to buy land and seeds, too," said the wife. "Then the ox can plow the land so we can plant the seeds."

So every night they would say,
"Moneybag, Moneybag,
Give us one silver piece."
And one silver piece would
roll out.

The pile of silver grew higher. "Let's buy the ox, land, and seeds now!" begged the husband.

"Not yet," answered his wife. "It's winter now. Let's wait until spring when we can plant the seeds."

So every night they would say,
"Moneybag, Moneybag,
Give us one silver piece."
And one silver piece would
roll out.

"Let's build a fine brick house!" cried the husband. "We can sell it, buy the ox, the land, and the seeds, and still have money left over."

Finally she agreed.

The husband bought bricks and lumber, and he hired bricklayers and carpenters.

From that day on, they did not cut firewood. They just sat and watched their house being built.

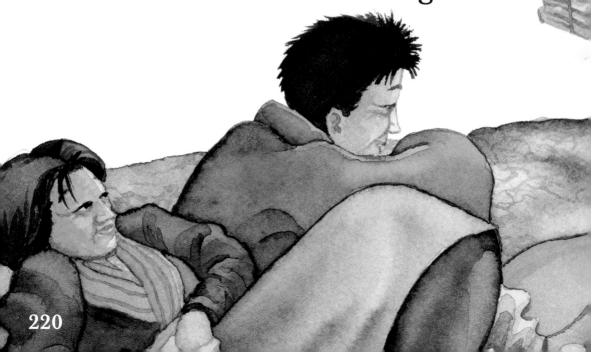

Before the house was finished, the silver was gone and so were the workers.

After his wife was asleep, the husband tiptoed to the moneybag and said,

"Moneybag, Moneybag,
Give me one silver piece."

And out rolled a silver piece.

Again he said,
"Moneybag, Moneybag,
Give me one silver piece."
And out rolled another
silver piece.

Greedily he said again,
"Moneybag, Moneybag,
Give me one silver piece."
But this time, no silver rolled
out. After several more tries, he
remembered the old man's words,
but it was too late.

His wife couldn't believe his
foolishness. "If we sell the house,
we may still have enough money
to buy an ox," she said.

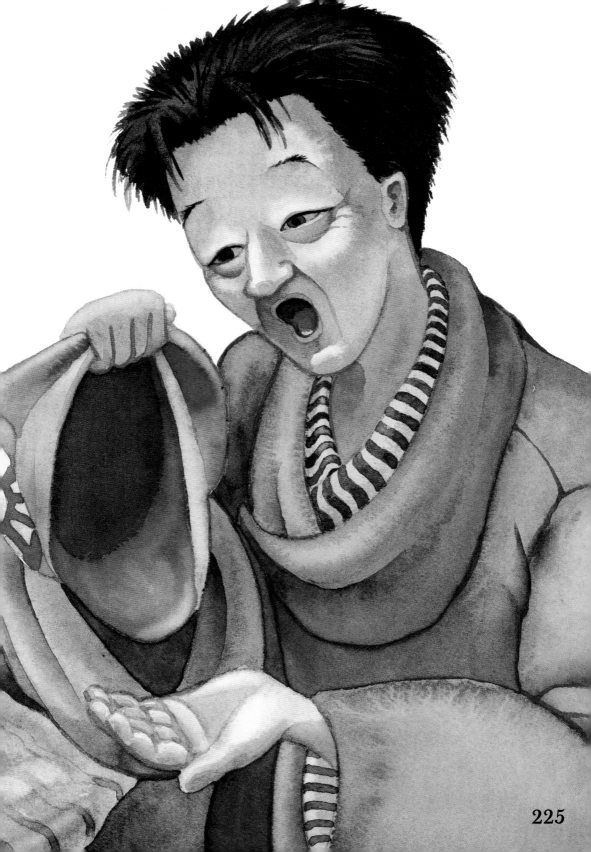

225

But when they awoke the next
morning, the couple's fine house
had disappeared.

They never forgot how greed lost them their good fortune. And for the rest of their lives, they cut firewood because they learned hard work would be the surest way to riches.

Beginning

Middle

End

Acknowledgments

Illustration Credits: Cartesia Software, Danielle Jones, Jeff Mangiat, Josée Masse, Jason O'Malley, Daniel Powers, Precision Graphics, Mike Reed, Three Communication Design, Jason Wolff.

Photo Credits: Page 6 (t) ©Steve Raymer/Corbis; 6 (c) ©Clifford Ober/Alamy; 6 (b) ©Liu Liqun/Corbis; 6-7 ©Richard Hutchings/Corbis; 10 ©Gerald French/Corbis; 10-13 Eric Camden; 15 ©Steve Raymer/Corbis; 16 (l) ©Kevin R. Morris/Bohemian Nomad Picturemakers/Corbis; 16 (r) ©Steve Raymer/Corbis; 16 (br) ©PhotoDisc/Getty Images; 17 ©Peter Turnley/Corbis; 18 Eric Camden; 19 ©Robert Frerck/Odyssey Productions, Inc./Chicago; 20 (br) ©Spike Mafford/Getty Images; 20 (c) ©John Dominis/Index Stock Imagery; 21 ©Ted Spiegel/Corbis; 22 Eric Camden; 23 ©Liu Liqun/Corbis; 24 Eric Camden; 25 ©Dennis Cox/China Stock; 25 (bl, br) Eric Camden; 26 Eric Camden; 27 ©Carl and Ann Purcell/Corbis; 28 (c) ©Alison Wright/Corbis; 28 (bl) ©PhotoDisc/Getty Images; 28 (cr) ©Alison Wright/Corbis; 29 ©Nik Wheeler/Corbis; 30 Eric Camden; 30 (bl) ©Mark E. Gibson/Corbis; 30 (tr) ©Jan Butchofsky-Houser/Corbis; 31 Eric Camden; 31 (tl, cr) ©PhotoDisc/Getty Images; 33 (Row 1,left) ©Kevin R. Morris/Bohemian Nomad Picturemakers/Corbis; 33 (Row1,2,3,4,center) Eric Camden; 33 (Row 2,left) ©John Dominis/Index Stock Imagery; 33 (Row 4,left) ©Alison Wright/Corbis; 33 (Row 2,right) ©Mark E. Gibson/Corbis; 33 (Row 1,right) ©Jan Butchofsky-Houser/Corbis; 33 (Row 3,right) ©PhotoDisc/Getty Images; 33 (Row 4,right) ©PhotoDisc/Getty Images; 33 (Row 3,left) ©Dennis Cox/China Stock; 34 (t) ©Corbis; 34 (c) ©Digital Vision/Getty Images; 34 (b) ©Corbis; 34-35 ©Odilon Dimier/age Fotostock; 62 (t) ©Hulton-Deutsch Collection/Corbis; 62 (c) ©Gianni Dagli Orti/Corbis; 62 (b) ©Hulton Archive/Getty Images; 62-63 ©Tim Bird/Corbis; 66-67 ©Tim Mendola for Jeff Mangiat; 67 (br) ©Sean Sexton Collection/Corbis; 68 ©Hulton-Deutsch Collection/Corbis; 69 ©Bettmann/Corbis; 70 ©David Turnley/Corbis; 70-71 (bgd) ©PhotoDisc/Getty Images; 71 ©Kevin R. Morris/Corbis; 72 (b) ©Gianni Dagli Orti/Corbis; 73 (c) ©The Granger Collection, New York; 73 (br) ©Hulton Archive/Getty Images; 74 (cl) ©North Wind Picture Archives; 74-75 ©Premium Stock/Corbis; 75 ©Michael S. Yamashita/Corbis; 76 (bl) ©Mireille Vautier/The Art Archive; 76-77 (c) ©Bettmann/Corbis; 77 (cr) ©Hulton Archive/Getty Images; 78 (c) ©Christie's Images/Corbis; 78-79 (bgd) ©PhotoDisc/Getty Images; 79 (c) ©AFP/Getty Images; 80 ©Bettmann/Corbis; 81 (c) ©Corbis; 81 (tr) ©Hulton Deutsch Collection/Corbis; 82 (cl) ©Eyewire/Getty Images; 82 (cr) ©Lester Lefkowitz/Corbis; 82-83 (bgd) ©Randy Faris/Corbis; 83 ©George Hall/Corbis; 83 (inset) ©PhotoDisc/Getty Images; 84 (bl) ©Bettmann/Corbis; 84-85 ©Corbis; 85 (br) ©Bettmann/Corbis; 85 (bl) ©Hulton Archive/Getty Images; 86 (cr) ©Reuters NewMedia Inc./Corbis; 86 (cl) ©Bettmann/Corbis; 86-87 (bgd) ©PhotoDisc/Getty Images; 87 (c) ©AFP/Getty Images; 88 (bgd) ©PhotoDisc/Getty Images; 89 (tl) ©Hulton-Duetsch Collection/Corbis; 89 (center 2 right) ©AFP/Getty Images; 89 (center 3 right) ©George Hall/Corbis; 89 (bgd left) ©PhotoDisc/Getty Images; 89 (br) ©AFP/ Getty; 89 (center 1 right) ©Michael S. Yamashita/Corbis; 89 (tr) ©Kevin R. Morris/Corbis; 89 (center 1 left) ©Gianni Dagli Orti/Corbis; 89 (center 2 left) ©Bettmann/Corbis; 89 (center 3 left) ©Corbis; 89 (bl) ©Corbis; 90 (b) ©Brand X/Jupiter Images; 90-91 ©Bounce/Getty Images; 122 ©Nik Wheeler/Corbis; 122 (c) ©NASA; 123 ©Jean-Michel Bertrand/Stockyard Photos; 124-125 ©David Graham; 126 ©NASA/JSC Digital Collection; 127 ©Roger Ressmeyer/Corbis; 128 ©Bob Gathany; 129 ©Richard T. Nowitz/Corbis; 130 ©NASA; 131 ©NASA; 132 ©Richard T. Nowitz/Corbis; 133 ©Bob Gathany; 135 ©Bob Gathany; 136 (l) ©Richard T. Nowitz/Corbis; 136 (r) ©Michael J. Doolittle/The Image Works; 137 ©Michael J. Doolittle/The Image Works; 139 (t) ©NASA/JSC Digital Image Collection; 139 (b) ©PhotoDisc/Getty Images; 140 (b) ©Michael J. Doolittle/The Image Works; 140 (tr) ©Robert Koropp; 141 ©Joseph Sohm/ChromoSohm/Corbis; 142 ©NASA/Kennedy Space Center Photo Archive; 143 ©Jonathan Nourok/PhotoEdit; 145 ©Joseph Sohm/ChromoSohm/Corbis; 145 (t) ©Jonathan Nourok/PhotoEdit; 145 (cl) ©NASA/JSC Digital Collection; 145 (cr) ©Richard T. Nowitz/Corbis; 145 (br) ©Michael J. Doolittle/The Image Works; 176 (c) ©Sharon Hoogstraten; 176-177 ©Brand X/Getty Images.